When Day Is Done

Nighttime Prayers through the Church Year

WHEN DAY is DONE

Nighttime Prayers
through the Church Year

Mark G. Boyer

TWENTY
THIRD 23rd
PUBLICATIONS

I dedicate this book to the
people of St. Francis of Assisi Parish
in Nixa, Missouri

Twenty-Third Publications
A Division of Bayard
One Montauk Avenue, Suite 200
New London, CT 06320
(860) 437-3012 or (800) 321-0411
www.23rdpublications.com

ISBN 978-1-58595-627-2
Library of Congress Catalog Card Number: 2006937648
Printed in the U.S.A.

✦ Contents

"Pray in the Spirit at all times in every prayer and supplication." So says St. Paul in his letter to the Ephesians (6:18).

In the Gospel of Luke, Jesus tells his disciples a parable about an unjust judge to illustrate "their need to pray always and not to lose heart" (18:1).

Both these passages express my goal for this book: to help you pray always—and especially at night by falling asleep with a prayer on your lips.

Nighttime prayer is an honored Christian tradition. Priests, brothers, and nuns are familiar with what once was called "Compline" in the Divine office. It is now referred to as "Night Prayer" in the Liturgy of the Hours. This liturgical prayer includes a hymn, an antiphon, psalm verses, a Scripture reading, a responsory, the gospel canticle from Luke 2:29–32, a concluding prayer, and an antiphon in honor of the Blessed Virgin Mary. It is meant to be the final prayer of the day. Because of its length, however, it does not meet the needs of most people today. (For those interested in exploring Night Prayer more fully, see the final section of this book.)

For those desiring a simpler form of night prayer, I offer selections here that correspond to the seasons of the liturgical year, but are simple and easy enough to be prayed in a minute or two. Each is an original prayer that echoes words from the psalms and other biblical writings.

My hope is that you will keep these prayers on a bed table or nightstand where you can easily reach them before turning out your light. Before you close your eyes to go to sleep, may a prayer be ever on your lips!

Note that in the prayers for Advent, I focus on two aspects of this season of anticipation: the second coming of Christ in glory and his incarnation.

My prayers for the Christmas season focus on the birth of Jesus, the Epiphany, and his baptism by John.

The lenten prayers echo the themes of prayer, fasting, and almsgiving and begin with Ash Wednesday and culminate on Holy Thursday when the Triduum begins. For the days of the Triduum, I offer prayers that reflect on the Eucharist, the Crucifixion, and on the light of Christ's resurrection.

My Easter prayers highlight the new life God offers during the fifty days of the Easter season.

The prayers for Ordinary Time offer general prayers that reflect many of the themes of the liturgy during this thirty-three to thirty-four week period.

Finally, I offer prayers for the feasts and solemnities of our Lord and for the solemnities of the saints as well.

Season
of Advent

Eternal God,
    always present even when I am not aware,
    make me joyful as I await the coming of Christ in glory.
Help me this Advent to break through the darkness of sin
    with the light of your grace,
    even as I now wrap myself in the sleep of this night
    with the hope of waking to the dawn of the next day.
Hear my prayer in the name of Jesus,
    the light of the world. Amen.

FIRST WEEK OF ADVENT

During this week, choose your night prayer from the following selections.

Mighty God,
 you sent Jesus among us to seek out what was lost.
Count me among those he has found
  when he comes again.
Produce in me the good works that will hasten his arrival.
Fill my mind with peaceful dreams of the kingdom
  where you live with Christ your Son and the Holy Spirit
  as one God, for ever and ever. Amen.

Lord God,
 you are rich in mercy and overflowing with forgiveness.
During these days of Advent, quiet my life.
Enable me to stand in awe of your presence
  as I prepare to celebrate the feast of the Incarnation.
Give me a peaceful night of sleep
  and permit me to awake to a new day
  of preparing for the coming of your Son,
Jesus Christ, who is Lord for ever and ever. Amen.

Good and upright Lord,
 you guide the humble to justice,
 you teach the humble your way.
Make your ways known to me this Advent.
Guide my footsteps in your truth.
Keep me in your peace this night.
Help me be ready for the coming in glory
  of your Son, Jesus Christ,
   who is Lord for ever and ever. Amen.

Holy One,
    you sent John the Baptist to prepare the way
        for your Son.
Help me make ready for his return in glory
    through my observance of Advent.
I desire to be found acceptable to you
    to whom, from whom, and for whom are all things
    this night and for ever and ever. Amen.

SECOND WEEK OF ADVENT

During this week, choose your night prayer from the following selections.

Father,
 you give me these days of Advent
 to wait in joyful hope
  for the coming of your Son in glory.
Instruct me in your ways
 that I may always walk in your paths.
May peace reign within the walls of my home this night.
I ask this in the name of Jesus the Lord. Amen.

God of justice,
 make right thought and right action
  flourish on the earth.
Make profound peace prevail throughout this Advent.
Remove anything from my life that hinders me
 from welcoming Christ with joy
  as I prepare to celebrate his birth.
Rest your hand upon me throughout this night.
Hear my prayer in the name of Jesus the Lord. Amen.

God of peace,
 your salvation draws near for those who revere you.
May your name be praised in this land.
Accept the words of praise from my lips this night.
You are God, living and true,
 with your Son, Jesus Christ,
 whose coming in glory I await,
 with the Holy Spirit, one God, for ever and ever. Amen.

Just One,
    you proclaim peace to your people;
    you announce that your salvation is near.
During these final days of Advent,
    rouse kindness, truth, and justice
        from deep within me.
During this night,
    bring forth from me a harvest of goodness
    as I prepare to celebrate the birth of your Son,
Jesus Christ, who is Lord for ever and ever. Amen.

During this week, choose your night prayer from the following selections.

I sing praise to you, faithful God.
    I give thanks to your holy name.
Throughout this day you have preserved my life;
    you have kept me in your love.
As the celebration of Christmas draws near,
    shine your face upon me even more
    and save me throughout this night.
I ask this through Christ, my Lord. Amen.

You reign forever, Lord God.
Through all generations your name is praised.
You secure justice for the oppressed,
    give food to the hungry,
    set captives free,
    give sight to the blind,
    and raise up those who are bowed down.
This night keep before me the advent of your Son,
    Jesus Christ, who is Lord for ever and ever. Amen.

Lord, my strength and courage,
    in you I am confident and unafraid this night.
I know that you are always with me.
I give you thanks for this season of Advent,
    and I proclaim how exalted is your name.
Receive my prayer of praise.
Make me ready for the coming of your Son, Jesus Christ,
    who is Lord for ever and ever. Amen.

Shepherd God,
    the earth and its fullness,
    the world and all who dwell in it, are yours.
Make my hands sinless and make my heart clean,
    that I may finish my Advent preparation
    by receiving a blessing from you.
As Christmas draws near,
    give me a night of peaceful rest.
Tomorrow, rouse your power and come to save me.
I ask this, Father, in the name of Jesus Christ, your Son,
    who lives and reigns with you and the Holy Spirit,
    one God, for ever and ever. Amen.

The Church recites the O Antiphons on the final days before Christmas. The following night prayers reflect this.

December 17, O Wisdom

God of wisdom,
    you guide all of creation with your power and love.
Bring justice to all afflicted people
    by endowing all leaders with knowledge of your ways.
Fill me with understanding that I may hear your Word
    and spread your peace throughout the world.
May your name be blessed this Advent night.
Hear my prayer in the name of Jesus Christ the Lord. Amen.

December 18, O Sacred Lord of Israel

God of Israel,
    you gave the law to Moses on Mount Sinai
    so that your people could live in security and peace.
Help me hear the cries of the poor;
    move me to rescue them through good works
    that I may experience your saving power
    as I prepare to celebrate the birth of your Son
    who ministered to the poor throughout his life.
Blessed forever be your name this night;
    may the whole earth be filled with your glory.
Hear me in the name of Jesus the Lord. Amen.

December 19, O Flower of Jesse's Stem

God of Jesse,
    through this servant of yours from Bethlehem
    you raised up King David as a sign of your love
      for your people.
In the fullness of time you raised up Jesus,
    the incarnation of your love for all peoples.
Make your love overflow through my life
    as I place my trust and hope in you this night.
Come without delay to save me
    through Jesus Christ my Lord. Amen.

December 20, O Key of David

God of King David,
    you ruled your people through a man
    of your own choosing.
But it was through your Son, the king of glory,
    that you opened the gates of your eternal kingdom.
Free me from any darkness
    that keeps Christ from coming into my heart
      this night.
Fill my dreams with the light of him
    who lives and reigns with you and the Holy Spirit,
    one God for ever and ever. Amen.

December 21, O Radiant Dawn

Mighty king and giver of light,
    your plan of creation stands forever,
    permeating every heart through all generations.
This night I sing you a new song in praise of Emmanuel
    who has come to save me.

As I await the celebration of his birth,
  make me rejoice and exult in your goodness.
I ask this through the holy name of Jesus Christ,
  who is Lord for ever and ever. Amen.

December 22, *O King of All the Nations*

Creator God, King of all the nations,
  out of the dust of the earth you fashioned me
  and filled me with countless blessings.
My soul proclaims your greatness
  and rejoices in your salvation.
Continue to do great things through me
  whether I am awake or asleep.
Holy is your name, Father, Son, and Holy Spirit,
  one God, for ever and ever. Amen.

December 23, *O Emmanuel*

Lord God, you have come among us
  through your Son, Jesus Christ, our Emmanuel.
As the feast of my redemption draws near,
  I lift up my heart in prayer to you.
May I always walk in your paths
    of kindness and constancy
  throughout the days and nights of my life.
Hear my prayer through Jesus Christ, your Son,
  the keystone of the church and Lord
    for ever and ever. Amen.

CHRISTMAS VIGIL

God, my rock,
   your favors are sung forever
   and through all generations
   by those who enter into covenant with you.
On this vigil of the birth of the Savior,
   I await tomorrow's radiant dawn
   when the splendor of eternal light
   will shine on all who dwell in darkness.
Throughout this night,
   maintain your goodness to me.
I ask this through Christ my Lord. Amen.

Season of Christmas

Redeeming God,
    today has been born the Savior of the world,
    your only-begotten Son, Christ the Lord.
Both heaven and earth have rejoiced
    as he came to rule the world with justice.
As I bring this day to a close,
    I praise you in the highest
    and pray for peace throughout the universe.
I ask this through my Lord Jesus Christ
    in the unity of the Holy Spirit,
    one God, for ever and ever. Amen.

....

Holy Family

Blessed are you, Lord God,
    giver of the human family.
Blessed are you in your Son, Jesus Christ,
    in his mother, the Blessed Virgin Mary,
    and in his foster father, Joseph.
Come and dwell in my house this night
    and protect me (and my family) from all harm
    with your shield of peace.
I ask this in the name of Jesus Christ, my Lord. Amen.

CHRISTMAS SEASON

During the days between Christmas and Epiphany, choose your night prayer from among the following selections.

Loving God,
   you announced salvation
   through the birth of your Son.
Glory to you in the highest
   for giving us the light that shatters the darkness.
Shine in my heart throughout this night
   as I rejoice through Jesus Christ, my Lord,
   in union with the Holy Spirit,
   one God, for ever and ever. Amen.

Lord God,
   your holy day dawned upon the world
   when your only-begotten Son
   was born of the Virgin Mary.
May all nations give you glory and praise
   for the great light that you have spread upon the earth.
May my sleep be a gift pleasing in your sight.
Hear my prayer through Jesus Christ, my Lord. Amen.

All of heaven and earth rejoice, O God,
   because your Word became flesh and dwelt among us.
Through him you have made me your child
   and anointed me with new life.
As I rest in peace this night,
   I sleep in confidence that Jesus' light
   shines in the darkness with grace and truth.
Continue to enlighten me from your fullness
   through Jesus Christ, my Lord. Amen.

Creator of heaven and earth,
   the celebration of the birth of your Son
   has been like holy light dawning upon the earth.
This evening I come before you with gladness,
   giving you thanks and blessing your name.
May your kindness endure throughout this night,
   and may your faithfulness bring me to a new day
      in your presence.
I make this prayer in the name of Jesus Christ, my Lord.
Amen.

Eternal God,
   your only-begotten Son became human
   that I might become one of your own sons
      and daughters.
Through my baptism into Christ's death and resurrection
   I already share in his divine nature.
Grant that through the remaining days and nights
      of my life,
   I may be conformed completely into his likeness
   and be found worthy of the kingdom of heaven,
      where he lives and reigns with you and the Holy Spirit,
         one God, for ever and ever. Amen.

Eternal Father,
    through the thick dark clouds of sin and death
    has shone your light of forgiveness and new life
    in the birth and manifestation of Jesus Christ, your Son.
Now, I bring him not gold, frankincense, and myrrh,
    but faith, hope, and love.
I ask you to let his star shine on me throughout this night
    and fill my dreams with his peace.
Hear my prayer in the name of him,
    who shares eternal unity with you and the Holy Spirit,
    for ever and ever. Amen.

THE DAYS AFTER EPIPHANY
AND BAPTISM OF THE LORD

Between Epiphany and the Baptism of the Lord, choose your night prayer from the following selections.

God of heaven and earth,
    your Son, Jesus Christ, proclaimed the gospel
      of your kingdom
    and manifested its presence by healing
    all who were sick and racked with pain.
Be with all who suffer from cancer;
    extend your healing touch to those
      recovering in hospitals
    and those preparing for surgery.
May all who sit in the darkness of illness
    discover the great light of your presence
    as I do this night.
I ask this through the divine physician, Jesus Christ,
    who is Lord for ever and ever. Amen.

God of plenty,
    through the ministry of your servant and your Son, Jesus,
    you fed thousands with a few loaves and fishes.
Bless those who serve the poor
    in soup kitchens and food pantries.
Move the hearts of others to share their wealth
    so that all your people may eat and be satisfied.
Help me bring your glad tidings to all I meet tomorrow
    after a night of plentiful rest in your presence.
Hear my prayer through Christ, my Lord. Amen.

Creator of the oceans,
  your Son revealed himself to his terrified disciples
  by walking on the waters of the sea.
When I am frightened, calm my soul with your Holy Spirit.
Give me the courage I need to lay down my head in sleep
  and rest throughout this night in your peace.
I ask this in the name of Jesus Christ,
  who is Lord for ever and ever. Amen.

May your name be blessed forever, mighty God.
May your name be remembered
      as long as the sun rises and sets.
Through your great mercy
  you brought to birth your Son, Jesus Christ,
  and manifested him to the nations.
I have seen his great light this day
  even as I now await the sleep of this night.
  Make me a better follower of him
  who has defeated death with eternal life,
Jesus Christ, who is Lord for ever and ever. Amen.

Saving God,
    your voice echoed over the waters
    as your Son was baptized in the Jordan River.
As you were pleased in him,
    be pleased with me as well
    for I have been baptized in water and your Holy Spirit.
On this last night of the Christmas season,
    wash me clean of my sins
    that I may sleep unafraid in peace
    and be confident that you are in my midst.
All holy One, hear my prayer
    through my Lord Jesus Christ,
    who lives with you and the Holy Spirit,
    one God, for ever and ever. Amen.

Season
of Lent

O Lord,
    you call me to return to you
        with my whole heart
    at the beginning of this season of Lent.
Have mercy on me in your goodness;
    wash me from my guilt and cleanse me of my sins.
Let the cross of ashes I have received this day
    be a sign of the clean heart you create for me
    and the steadfast spirit you renew within me.
Let my almsgiving, prayer, and fasting
    soften my heart
    so that my every breath this night
    will give you praise: Father, Son, and Holy Spirit,
    one God, for ever and ever. Amen.

Choose your night prayer from the following selections.

God of Abraham, Isaac, and Jacob,
  your patriarchs delighted in your ways
  and meditated on your law day and night.
Make me like a tree planted near running water,
  prospering in your grace
  and yielding abundant fruit during this lenten season.
May the words of your law be in my mind and heart
    this night
  as I place all my hope in you.
Hear my prayer
  in the name of your Son, Jesus Christ, my Lord. Amen.

Lord God,
  have mercy on me in your goodness.
Out of the greatness of your compassion
  turn my selfishness to altruism this Lent
  through prayer, fasting, and almsgiving.
You have cleansed me from sin
  in the saving waters of baptism.
Renew in me a heart contrite and humbled
  throughout the rest of this night.
I ask this in the name of Jesus Christ, my Lord. Amen.

Good and upright Lord,
  you show sinners the way;
  you guide the humble to justice.
Make your ways known to me;
  teach me to walk the paths of your truth this Lent.
Overwhelm me with your love and compassion,
  with your kindness and goodness.
Let no evil befall me this night.
  I ask this in the name of Jesus Christ, my Lord,
  who lives and reigns with you, Father and Holy Spirit,
  one God, for ever and ever. Amen.

During this week, choose your night prayer from the following selections.

Merciful God,
   incline your ear toward me,
   hear my prayer, and answer me.
I confess my sins to you and beg for your forgiveness.
Through my lenten practices
   gladden my soul and help me walk in your truth.
Keep me safe throughout this night
   as I place all my trust in you.
Attend to the sound of my prayer
   in the name of Jesus Christ, my Lord. Amen.

I glorify your name, Lord God.
Every time I seek you, you answer me.
Through my lenten fasting
   make me aware of the hunger of the poor.
Through my almsgiving
   put me in solidarity with the suffering.
Through my prayer
   bring me close to the brokenhearted.
Deliver me from all my fears this night
   and make me radiant with the joy of the Holy Spirit,
   who with you and Jesus Christ are one God,
   for ever and ever. Amen.

Almighty Father,
   out of the dark depths of the night I cry to you.
Hear my voice and be attentive to my prayer.
Fill me with your forgiveness during this Lent.
Help me trust more in your Word
   and wait for you to act in my daily life.
Let the words of my mouth and the thoughts of my heart
   find favor before you this night, O Lord, my rock.
Hear my prayer through Jesus Christ,
      my redeemer and Lord. Amen.

Creator God,
    the earth is full of your kindness.
Hear the sound of my call,
    have pity on me and answer me.
During this season of Lent,
    make your light of grace grow stronger within me
    and bring to completion
        the salvation you have begun in me.
This night deliver me from death and preserve me
    as I put my hope in you.
I ask this through my Lord Jesus Christ,
    who lives and reigns with you, Father and Holy Spirit,
    one God, for ever and ever. Amen.

During this week, choose your night prayer from the following selections.

I seek your presence, O Lord;
    hide not your face from me.
Do not remember my sins
    but shower me with your forgiveness.
Throughout Lent, help me spread reconciliation.
I wait for you with courage throughout this night,
    believing that tomorrow I shall see
    your bounty in the land of the living.
I place my trust in you
    through Jesus Christ, my Lord. Amen.

Merciful God,
    you create a new heart and a new spirit
    in me through my observance of Lent.
May my prayer, fasting, and almsgiving
    renew my baptismal covenant with you.
I place my destiny in your hands this night,
    trusting that you will rescue me in your kindness.
Hear my prayer through Jesus Christ, my Lord. Amen.

As I prepare for a night of rest and sleep,
    I remember the marvels you have done, Mighty God.
You have pardoned my sins,
    healed my illnesses,
    redeemed my life from destruction,
    and crowned me with kindness and compassion.
All my being blesses your holy name.
Throughout Lent, help me remember your goodness.
Accept my thanks through your Son, Jesus Christ,
    who lives and reigns with you and the Holy Spirit,
    one God, for ever and ever. Amen.

Merciful and gracious God,
    you are slow to anger and abounding in kindness.
I come bowing down in worship before you this night.
Through the waters of baptism
    you made me your son/daughter,
    and you guide me with your Holy Spirit to eternal life.
During this lenten season,
    help me hear your voice with an open heart.
I come into your presence with this prayer of thanksgiving
    through Jesus Christ, your Son,
        who is Lord for ever and ever. Amen.

During this week, choose your night prayer from the following selections.

As far as the east is from the west,
  you put my sins from me, forgiving God.
I long for the running streams of your grace;
  I thirst for you, my living God.
Send forth your light and your fidelity this night;
  they shall lead me through this season of repentance
  to the holy mountain of new life
  lavished upon me through Jesus Christ, your Son,
  who is Lord for ever and ever. Amen.

God of gladness and joy,
  I have been to your altar to give you thanks
  for all that you have done in my life.
Continue to teach me your ways
  through the lenten disciplines
    of prayer, fasting, and almsgiving.
Remember your mercies throughout this night.
I ask this through Jesus Christ, my Lord. Amen.

Eternal God,
    you send your Word to the earth
    that I might know and walk in your ways.
During this time of lenten fasting,
    feed me with the best of wheat
        and with honey from the rock.
Renew in me the promises I made in baptism.
Make my thoughts this night acceptable to you,
    my rock and redeemer,
    through Jesus Christ, my Lord,
    who lives with you in the unity of the Holy Spirit,
    one God, for ever and ever. Amen.

Shepherd God, I want for nothing.
You lead me to restful waters and verdant pastures.
You guide me in right paths with your Word.
This day you have spread the eucharistic table before me.
Your goodness and kindness follow me
    all the days of my life.
I bless you at all times,
    but especially during this lenten season.
May your praise be ever in my mouth this night
    through Jesus Christ, your Son,
      in union with the Holy Spirit, one God,
        for ever and ever. Amen.

FOURTH WEEK OF LENT

During this week, choose your night prayer from the following selections.

Lord of hosts,
    my refuge and strength,
    my ever-present help in distress,
    you preserve my life and keep me safe.
Raise my awareness of your constant presence
    and create in me a new heart during this Lent
    that I may trust more deeply in you.
Hear my prayer this night in the name of Jesus Christ,
      your Son,
    who is Lord for ever and ever. Amen.

Eternal God,
    your kindness is from eternity to eternity
    toward those who fear you.
Your justice is everlasting
    for those who keep your covenant.
Pour out your compassion on me this Lent.
Remember that I am formed from the dust of the earth
    and to that dust I will one day return.
May my sleep bless your name throughout this night.
I ask this in the name of Jesus Christ, your Son,
    who is Lord for ever and ever. Amen.

Great are you, Lord God, and wholly to be praised
   for the great mercy you show your sinful people.
During this time of Lent,
      you urge me to return to you
         with prayer, fasting, and almsgiving
      that I might renew with you my covenant
         begun in baptism.
Deepen my prayer,
      strengthen my fasting,
      and enliven my almsgiving.
Throughout this night may your name be praised
      to the ends of the earth
      through Jesus Christ, your Son, and the Holy Spirit,
      who live and reign with you for ever and ever. Amen.

God of life and death,
    open your ears in attention to my prayer.
I have strayed from you and done what is evil in your sight.
In your kindness create in me a clean heart
    and shower me with your forgiveness this Lent.
I make this prayer in trust of your Word this night
    awaiting the dawn of your plenteous redemption
    through Jesus Christ, my Lord,
      who lives and reigns with you and the Holy Spirit,
      one God for ever and ever. Amen.

During this week, choose your night prayer from the following selections.

Hear my cry, Lord God,
    and hearken to my prayer from truthful lips.
You are rich in mercy
    and you save those who flee to you.
During this last week of Lent,
    make me more and more aware of your saving power.
Hide me in the shadow of your wings this night
    that I may awake content in your presence.
I ask this in the name of Jesus Christ, my Lord. Amen.

O Searcher of heart and soul,
    you shined the light of your face
    on countless men and women of the past
    who kept your covenant and did your will.
Hide not your face from me.
Keep me faithful to my baptismal promises
    and guide me through these final days of Lent
    to more deeply understand your ways.
Hear my prayer, O God, this night
    and let my cry come to you
    through Jesus Christ, your Son,
    who is Lord for ever and ever. Amen.

Eternal Father,
    blessed is your holy and glorious name.
Blessed are you in the outermost reaches of the universe.
Blessed are you in the hearts of all believers.
Grant that I may never cease to praise you
    and exalt your name throughout this night.
Bring me through these last days of Lent
    to the new life you promise.
I ask this in the name of Jesus Christ, my Lord. Amen.

Passion Sunday (Palm Sunday)

Hosanna in the highest, mighty God.
Your Son, my Lord Jesus Christ,
    came in your name
    while people waved palms of victory before him.
This day in the midst of the assembly
    I have remembered his triumphal entrance
        into Jerusalem
    and his suffering and death that followed on the cross.
With great praise this night I proclaim your holy name.
In union with the Holy Spirit, I confess
    that Jesus Christ is Lord to your glory, Father,
        for ever and ever. Amen.

Monday, Tuesday, Wednesday of Holy Week

God of light and salvation,
    you have been my refuge from my mother's womb.
When the evil of darkness comes near,
    your light dispels my fear and saves me from all harm.
Trusting that I shall see your bounty
        in the land of the living,
    I put my life in your hands this night.
Be my stronghold of safety throughout this holy week
    that I may sing of your salvation:
Father, Son, and Holy Spirit, one God,
        for ever and ever. Amen.

Holy Thursday

Lord Jesus Christ,
    you taught your followers
    to offer the sacrifice of thanksgiving
       of your body and blood
    in the presence of your people.
Then, you commanded them to love one another
    as you have loved all to your death on the cross.
On this Holy Thursday,
    I have eaten the bread of your body
    and shared the saving cup of your blood.
Help me imitate your love.
This night grant that my sleep proclaims your death
    until you come in the glory that you share
    with the Father in the unity of the Holy Spirit,
    one God, for ever and ever. Amen.

Good Friday

Faithful God,
    your only-begotten Son, my Lord Jesus Christ,
    was obedient to you to the point of death,
    even death on a cross.
As I have celebrated his passion this day,
    trace in my life the lines of his faith.
Throughout this night
    let your face shine upon me, your servant;
    save me in your kindness
    as you greatly exalted Jesus Christ
    and bestowed on him the name
    which is above every other name
    and made him Lord for ever and ever. Amen.

Holy Saturday

Saving God,
    you have brightened the darkness of this night
    with the glory of Christ's resurrection
    and sent out your Holy Spirit to renew the face
        of the earth.
I have remembered your work of creation,
    your promises to Abraham and Sarah,
    your redemption of Israel at the Red Sea,
    and the clean water you sprinkled on your people.
Grant that my lenten prayer, fasting, and almsgiving
    be as a baptism into the death of Christ
    so that I may rise with him to newness of life
    and declare your works through my waking and sleeping.
I give thanks to you, Father,
    through Jesus Christ, your Son,
    who lives and reigns with you and the Holy Spirit,
    one God, for ever and ever. Amen.
    Alleluia! Alleluia!

Season
of Easter

Good and gracious God,
    your mercy endures forever.
Your right hand of power
    struck the sealed tomb of Jesus
    and released him from the bonds of death.
Now he lives to declare your works.
May I never cease to rejoice and be glad
    in the new life you have given me
    through my baptism
        into the death and resurrection of Christ,
    the paschal lamb who has taken away the sins
        of the world.
Now that I have celebrated this Easter Sunday with joy,
    grant me a night of peaceful sleep
    as I put all my hope in you:
Father, Son, and Holy Spirit,
    one God, for ever and ever. Amen.
    Alleluia! Alleluia!

During this week, choose your night prayer from the following selections.

Lord God,
    you make my heart glad and my soul rejoice
    as I celebrate the resurrection of Jesus Christ, your Son.
I can abide in confidence this night,
    because you will not abandon me to the netherworld
    nor will you let me undergo corruption.
Counsel me throughout my sleep
    and exhort me as I walk the path of life in your presence.
I ask this through Jesus Christ, my Lord. Amen.
    Alleluia! Alleluia!

I give thanks to you and invoke your name, mighty God.
I praise you and proclaim your wondrous deeds.
On the darkness of the grave
    you have shed the light of your glory
    and filled the earth with your goodness.
Look upon me this night
    and deliver me from death.
May your kindness be upon me
    as I put all my hope in you, Father,
    with your Son, Jesus Christ, and the Holy Spirit,
    one God, for ever and ever. Amen.
    Alleluia! Alleluia!

O Lord, my God,
    how glorious is your name over all the earth.
Once you created everything that is,
    but through the resurrection of Jesus Christ
    you have re-created everything and made all new.
Through the waters of baptism
    you have crowned me with glory and honor
    and given me rule over the works of your hands.
Give me a restful night in your presence.
I ask this in the name of Jesus Christ,
    who is Lord for ever and ever. Amen.
    Alleluia! Alleluia!

Saving God, whose mercy endures forever,
  when I had sinned and wandered far from
    your covenant,
  you brought me back to you
    through the death of your Son.
Be my strength and courage when I fall.
You have given me this day of resurrection,
  and my heart is filled with gladness
  and rejoicing in your sight.
Keep me in your everlasting love throughout this night.
I ask this in the name of Jesus Christ, your Son,
  who lives and reigns with you and the Holy Spirit,
  one God, for ever and ever. Amen.
  Alleluia! Alleluia!

SECOND WEEK OF EASTER

During this week, choose your night prayer from the following selections.

Merciful God,
I give thanks to you for raising Jesus Christ from the dead.
You made him, the stone rejected by the builders,
    the cornerstone of your church.
As you have filled me
        with the joy of Christ's resurrection this day,
        grant me the confidence of salvation this night.
I ask this in the name of Jesus Christ, my Lord. Amen.
    Alleluia!

O Lord, my king,
    for length of days, you have been robed
        in splendor and strength.
You anointed Jesus Christ, your Son, with the oil of gladness
    by raising him from the death he suffered on the cross.
Through my baptism
    I now share in the eternal life he lives with you.
Guide me as I seek what is above
    where Christ is seated at your right hand.
Give me rest as I pause this night on my journey.
Hear my prayer through Jesus Christ, my Lord. Amen.
    Alleluia!

Eternal God,
  you answer those who seek you
  and you deliver them from all their fears.
I look to you that I may be radiant with joy
  and that my face may never blush with shame.
Grant that I may bless you at all times,
  especially throughout this night,
  that your praise may ever be in my mouth
  through my Lord Jesus Christ, your risen Son,
  who lives and reigns with you and the Holy Spirit,
  one God, for ever and ever. Amen.
  Alleluia!

Almighty God,
    your spotless, unblemished Lamb, Jesus Christ,
    has ransomed me with his precious blood.
My heart is glad and my soul rejoices in this wonderful gift.
Continue to show me the path to life
    and give me abounding joy in your presence
    throughout these fifty days of Easter.
As soon as I lie down, grant that I may fall asleep peacefully,
    for you alone bring me security,
Father, Son, and Holy Spirit, for ever. Amen.
    Alleluia!

THIRD WEEK OF EASTER

During this week, choose your night prayer from the following selections.

You, Lord, are my light and my salvation.
I fear no one nor any thing.
I seek you and ask only one favor:
    To dwell in your presence all the days of my life
    that I might recognize your loveliness in all creation.
Grant me a night of rest and watch over me until the dawn.
I ask this in the name of your Son,
    Jesus Christ, my Lord. Amen.
    Alleluia!

O God, my rock of refuge,
    you are the stronghold that gives me safety
    as you lead and guide me throughout
        my lifetime journey.
I put all my trust in you because of your mercy.
Let your face shine upon me;
    hide me in the shelter of your presence this night.
Into your hands I commend my spirit.
Hear my prayer, Father, in the name of Jesus Christ,
    who lives and reigns with you and the Holy Spirit,
    one God, for ever and ever. Amen.
    Alleluia!

Blessed are you, Lord God,
     who shows me kindness and answers my prayers.
All the earth sings praise to you.
You changed the sea into dry land
     so that your chosen people could escape slavery.
You raised Christ from the dead
     so that your people could escape sin.
I place my confidence in you this night
     for your fidelity endures forever.
Hear my prayer through Jesus Christ, my Lord. Amen.
     Alleluia!

Holy One, my good shepherd,
  beside restful waters you lead me to refresh my soul.
You guide me in right paths
  even when I walk through the dark valley.
Your goodness and kindness follow me
    all the days of my life.
You tend me like a shepherd watching over his sheep.
Give me repose in verdant pastures this night
  as I place all my hope in your faithfulness.
I ask this, Father, through my Lord Jesus Christ, your Son,
  who lives and reigns with you and the Holy Spirit,
  one God, for ever and ever. Amen.
  Alleluia!

During this week, choose your night prayer from the following selections.

Living God,
    my soul longs for you like the deer longs
        for running waters.
You never forget any thing that you have created.
You have sent forth your stream of grace on the earth
    through the resurrection of Jesus Christ.
Throughout my days and nights
    help me drink deeply of the river of life
    that will lead me to your holy mountain,
    your dwelling place in heaven,
    where you live and reign with your Son
    and the Holy Spirit for ever and ever. Amen.
Alleluia!

Mighty God,
    you make the nations glad and exultant
    with the mercy you have shown all people
    through the death and resurrection of your Son.
Help me know your ways upon earth
    that I may share in the blessings of salvation.
Grant that all people may praise you as I do this night.
Bless me through Jesus Christ my Lord. Amen.
    Alleluia!

Eternal God,
 all the ends of the earth have seen your saving power
 through the wondrous resurrection of Christ your Son.
In him you have remembered your kindness
  and faithfulness
 toward all your creation.
As I prepare for sleep this night,
 I sing you a new song;
 I praise the power of your right hand;
 I acknowledge your favors through all generations.
Hear my prayer of praise in the name of Jesus Christ,
 who is Lord for ever and ever. Amen.
 Alleluia!

Lord God,
    you are gracious and merciful,
    slow to anger and of great kindness.
You are compassionate toward all your works.
This night I bow before you and give you thanks
    for raising your Son, Jesus Christ, from the dead
    and bestowing through him new life on all creation.
May all the living praise you.
May all the dead honor you.
May I live only for you, Father,
    through your Son, in union with the Holy Spirit,
    for ever and ever. Amen.
    Alleluia!

FIFTH WEEK OF EASTER

During this week, choose your night prayer from the following selections.

God in heaven,
    whatever you will, you do.
I give glory to you because of the mercy and truth
    you have revealed through the resurrection of Jesus Christ.
Maker of heaven and earth,
      may all your works give you thanks;
      may all people bless you.
May my mouth speak your praises this night,
    and may all flesh bless your holy name
    through your Son, who lives and reigns with you
      and the Holy Spirit,
    one God, for ever and ever. Amen.
    Alleluia!

Lord God,
    you established King David over the tribes of Israel
    to form them into the community of your chosen people.
Through the death and resurrection of Jesus Christ
    you established your Son as king over all people
    to guide them to the new Jerusalem of eternal life.
For all your wondrous deeds I sing a new song to you.
I bless your name this night
    in the trust that you will allow me to set foot
      within the gates
    of the holy city where you live
      and reign for ever and ever. Amen.
    Alleluia!

I give thanks to you, steadfast God.
I chant your praises throughout my days and nights.
Your mercy towers to the heavens;
   your faithfulness, demonstrated
      in the resurrection of Christ,
   is greater than the skies.
Grant that after a night of rest I may awake at dawn
   singing your praises: Father, Son, and Holy Spirit,
   one God living for ever and ever. Amen.
   Alleluia!

Saving God,
   you never forget your kindness and faithfulness.
You have revealed your salvation to the ends of the earth.
I declare what you have done for me:
   through the waters of baptism
   you have plunged me into
   the death and resurrection of Jesus Christ.
How tremendous are your deeds!
Before I go to sleep,
   I shout praise to the glory of your name.
Have pity on me, bless me,
   and let your face shine upon me throughout this night.
Father, I ask this in the name of Jesus Christ, your Son,
   who lives and reigns with you and the Holy Spirit,
   one God, for ever and ever. Amen.
   Alleluia!

THE ASCENSION

Mighty God,
   you are the great king over all the earth.
You reign over all the nations from your holy throne.
With shouts of joy and trumpet blasts
   you raised your Son, Jesus Christ, from the dead
   and seated him with you in glory.
As I have celebrated his ascension into heaven,
   grant me the confidence throughout this night
   that one day you will raise me to the new life
   which you share with my Lord Jesus Christ
   and the Holy Spirit, for ever and ever. Amen.
   Alleluia!

During this week, choose your night prayer from the following selections.

Loving God,
   your right hand has saved me from death
   through the resurrection of your Son, Jesus Christ.
For that great deed I sing your praises and exult in glory.
Because of your kindness and your truth,
   you will protect me throughout this night.
Tomorrow, I trust that you will complete even more
   what you have done for me
   through Jesus Christ, who is Lord for ever and ever. Amen.
   Alleluia!

Holy One, all the ends of the earth have seen your salvation
   through the death and resurrection of Jesus Christ.
All creation praises you for your gift of the Holy Spirit.
This night I join my voice
   to that of presidents and prime ministers,
   kings and queens, old men and old women,
   young men and young women, boys and girls.
Your name alone is exalted
   through your Son, Jesus Christ,
   who lives and reigns with you and the Holy Spirit,
one God, for ever and ever. Amen.
   Alleluia!

Most High Lord,
    all people clap their hands in joy
    and shout to you with cries of gladness
    at the resurrection of Jesus Christ.
Tonight I offer you this prayer of praise
    for all the gifts that you have bestowed upon me this day,
    both those I have recognized
        and those that have gone unnoticed.
Accept my praises through my Lord Jesus Christ,
    who lives with you and the Holy Spirit,
    one God, for ever and ever. Amen.
    Alleluia!

SEVENTH SUNDAY OF EASTER

(See The Ascension on page 64.)

Most High Lord,
   the heavens proclaim your justice
   while all people see your mighty benefits.
As far as the east is from the west,
   so far have you put my transgressions from your sight.
Hear the sound of my call this night;
   have pity on me and answer me.
Enlighten my darkness with the light of your salvation.
I ask this, Father, through Jesus Christ,
   who with you and the Holy Spirit are one God,
   for ever and ever. Amen.

SEVENTH WEEK OF EASTER

During this week, choose your night prayer from the following selections.

Blessed day by day are you, O Lord.
You save me from sin
    through the death and resurrection of Jesus Christ.
You save me from death
    through the gift of the Holy Spirit.
As you have helped me bear the burdens of this day,
    so come to my aid this night.
I praise your name through your Son
    in the unity of the Holy Spirit, one God,
    for ever and ever. Amen.
    Alleluia!

Send forth, O God, the power of your Spirit
    to give me strength to praise you for this day.
You have kept me safe
    as I have taken refuge in you.
This night I set you before me,
    trusting that your right hand will protect me.
Counsel me even through my sleep
    and let my heart ever praise you
    through Jesus Christ, whom you raised from the dead,
    who is Lord for ever and ever. Amen.
    Alleluia!

God of power and might,
    you search my heart with your Holy Spirit
    and discern the thoughts of my mind.
Your kindness to me surpasses understanding.
I bless your holy name this night.
Shine your face upon me and
    keep me in your peace.
Hear this prayer through Jesus Christ, my Lord. Amen.
    Alleluia!

Father of my Lord Jesus Christ,
    you did not permit your Son to remain
        in the sleep of death
    for you awakened him to the dawn of eternal life
        through the power of your Holy Spirit.
How manifold are all your works!
How wise are all your decisions!
Send the Advocate to me:
    renew me with the Spirit's breath;
    fill me with the Spirit's fire;
    guide me with the Spirit's love.
Make me an instrument of Pentecost
    as I bless your name this night
    through Jesus Christ, your Son,
    who lives and reigns with you and the Holy Spirit,
    one God, for ever and ever. Amen.
    Alleluia! Alleluia!

Season of
Ordinary Time

God, in every time and place, in all of your creation,
    you have revealed the light of your glory.
I have looked upon the image of Jesus Christ
    in the countless faces I have seen this day.
Give me a night of rest
    and lead me to a deeper understanding of your truth
    as I arise tomorrow to praise you:
Father, Son, and Holy Spirit,
    one God, for ever and ever. Amen.

Mighty God,
    you have manifested your presence to me
    in all creation and in the people I have met
    as I made my way through the hours of this day.
I have run the race and kept the faith
    and come to this night in the hope
    of rising again to praise you:
Father, Son, and Holy Spirit,
    one God, for ever and ever. Amen.

Faithful God,
    in all I have done this day
    I know you have been with me,
    whether I was aware of it or not.
I do believe in you and trust you.
Help my unbelief and lack of trust.
Strengthen me for your service through this night of rest.
I ask this through Jesus Christ, my Lord. Amen.

God of day and night,
    you have brought me safely through this day.
Now be with me through this night.
Surround me with your mighty power;
    preserve me from all sin;
    protect me from all adversity.
Through my sleep
    direct me to the fulfillment of your purposes.
I ask this through Jesus Christ, my Lord. Amen.

Creator God,
    you formed people in your own image
    and set them over the whole world in all its wonder.
Give me, your creature, a restful night.
Bless me with an awareness of your presence
    in the east and in the west, in the north and in the south.
May your peace abide in my house this night.
Hear my prayer through Christ, my Lord. Amen.

Lord God,
    your mercy extends from east to west
    and from north to south over all the earth.
Though this day is now finished,
    I ask you to protect and defend me throughout the night.
Keep away all evil,
    grant me peaceful rest,
    and awaken me to a new day in your presence.
I ask this in the name of Jesus Christ, my Lord. Amen.

Good and upright Lord,
    you guide me in your truth and teach me.
You show me your ways.
Remember your compassion this night;
    hold none of my transgressions against me.
In your kindness remember me
    and keep me safe.
Hear my prayer through Jesus Christ,
    who lives and reigns with you and the Holy Spirit,
    one God, for ever and ever. Amen.

Lord,
    your law is perfect;
    your decrees are trustworthy;
    your precepts are right;
    your commands are clear;
    your ordinances are true.
Forgive the ways that I may have strayed this day.
Give me simple wisdom, a rejoicing heart,
        an enlightened eye.
May the words of my mouth and the thoughts of my heart
    find favor before you this night.
I ask this in the name of Jesus Christ, my Lord. Amen.

Lord God,
    I come into your presence with thanksgiving,
    praising you for the salvation you have given me this day.
I bow in worship before you;
    I kneel before you who made me.
Be my stronghold of safety throughout this night.
Be my rock of refuge as I rest in peace.

I have depended upon you from my mother's womb.
Hear my proclamation of your wondrous deeds
through Jesus Christ, my Lord,
who lives with you and the Holy Spirit,
one God, for ever and ever. Amen.

Eternal God,
you are gracious, merciful, and just.
As I have enjoyed your grace, mercy, and truth this day,
I lie down in peace with the hope
that sleep will come at once.
Make my heart firm, always trusting in you.
Keep me in your safety throughout this night.
I ask this in your name, Father,
through my Lord Jesus Christ, your Son,
who lives and reigns with you and the Holy Spirit,
one God, for ever and ever. Amen.

Saving God,
I give you thanks with all my heart
for you have heard the words of my mouth.
When I called, you answered me
and built up strength within me.
Before I rest in peace
I lift up my voice in blessing this night.
Tomorrow, complete the good work you have begun in me
through your Son, Jesus Christ,
who lives and reigns with you
in the unity of your Holy Spirit,
one God, for ever and ever. Amen.

Blessed may you be, O Lord, from all eternity.
You instruct me in your ways
   that I may walk in your paths.
You give me discernment
   that I may observe your law with all my heart.
Be good to your servant
   that I may rest throughout this night.
At dawn, open my eyes
   that I may consider the wonders of your presence.
Hear this prayer in the name of Jesus Christ, my Lord. Amen.

Lord God,
   you may let your servant rest in peace.
I have seen your Word fulfilled this day.
With my own eyes I have viewed your salvation.
Only in you can I be at rest,
   for you alone are the rock of my strength and my refuge.
I trust that I will not be disturbed.
Hear my prayer through Christ, my Lord. Amen.

Creator God,
   how manifold are the works of your hand.
You formed the planets and set them on their courses.
You covered the earth with the oceans,
   making the mountains point toward your glory.
Give me a greater appreciation for your handiwork
   after this night of rest.
Blessed are you, Father, Son, and Holy Spirit,
   one God, for ever and ever. Amen.

God of all,
    you created the human family to serve you
    by filling the earth and managing its resources.
Bless all men and fathers this night.
Bless all women and mothers this night.
Bless all children this night.
May you be blessed in my resting and rising.
Hear my prayer in the name of Jesus Christ,
    who is Lord for ever and ever. Amen.

From the rising of the sun to its setting, O Lord,
    you are worthy of all praise.
May those who have lived before me,
    those who inhabit the earth now,
    and all future generations praise you.
Before I sleep this night,
    I call upon all creation to give you the glory
        due your name:
    Father, Son, and Holy Spirit,
        one God living for ever and ever. Amen.

Sheltering God,
    those who live in your shadow
    find refuge under your wings.
I do not fear the terror of the night
    for I trust in your faithfulness.
Send your angels to keep me in your ways.
I ask this in the name of Jesus Christ, your Son,
    who lives and reigns with you and the Holy Spirit,
    one God, for ever and ever. Amen.

Lord God, you are good and forgiving,
    full of love to all who call upon you.
Listen to my prayer and attend to the sound of my voice.
Preserve my life this night,
    for I am a faithful servant who trusts in you.
Have mercy upon me
    as I lift up my soul to you.
Hear my prayer in the name of Jesus Christ, my Lord. Amen.

Eternal God,
    you live in perfect love with your Son, Jesus Christ,
    and the Holy Spirit.
Fill my heart with your love.
Teach me to do your will.
Let your Holy Spirit guide me
    in ways that are level and smooth.
After a night of rest,
    let me know your love again in the morning
    as I place all my trust in you:
    one God for ever and ever. Amen.

Faithful God,
    as I wait for you to reveal your presence to me,
    I count on your Word and your forgiveness.
This night I pray from the depths of my inmost being.
Hear my voice and be attentive to my pleading.
Shine your face upon me
    throughout the darkness of the night.
I long for you like those who watch the eastern sky
    for the first rays of dawn.
Hear my prayer through Jesus Christ, my Lord. Amen.

Father, Son, and Holy Spirit,
    you have shown me the path of life this day,
    the fullness of joy and happiness in your presence.
Accept the work I have done this day
    and throughout the night counsel my heart
    that I may arise with renewed faith and love.
Father, Son, and Holy Spirit, one God, for ever and ever.
Amen.

Merciful Father,
    as I have called for your help this day,
    I now bring my prayer to you this night.
Let my prayers come into your presence.
Bless all who have found fault with me this day.
Bless all with whom I have found fault this day.
May your forgiveness and peace flow from my home
    into the neighborhood and out into the whole world.
Banish all evil from this place
    and send your blessings upon me.
I ask this in the name of Jesus Christ, my Lord. Amen.

Every day and night I bless you, Lord God,
    I praise your name forever and ever.
You are great and highly to be praised;
    your greatness is unsearchable.
May all your works give you thanks
    and may all your faithful people bless you,
    as I do this night.
All power and glory be yours, Father, Son, and Holy Spirit,
    one God for ever and ever. Amen.

Saving God,
>   you watch over the lives of your people,
>   keeping them in your loving embrace.
> Strengthen my trust in you
>   and help me to do good every day of my life.
> I long for your salvation throughout this night.
> Let me live to praise you tomorrow
>   through Jesus Christ, your Son,
>   who lives and reigns with you and the Holy Spirit,
>   one God, for ever and ever. Amen.

Your kindness, O Lord, is from eternity to eternity
>   toward those who keep your covenant.
> You formed me from the dust of the earth
>   and showered me with your boundless compassion.
> My days and nights are numbered in your presence.
> Teach me discernment, and in your mercy
>   preserve my life this night.
> Hear my prayer in the name of Jesus Christ, my Lord. Amen.

Creator God,
>   upright is your Word and trustworthy are all your works.
> You formed the heavens and the earth,
>   gathering the waters of the seas
>   and creating people in your own image and likeness.
> I give thanks to you for the marvels of creation,
>   especially all those I have witnessed this day.
> Remember your compassion and kindness this night
>   and grant me a peaceful rest.
> Hear my prayer through Jesus Christ, my Lord. Amen.

Eternal God,
　　I bless you at all times and extol your name.
When I pray to you, you answer me.
When I seek you, you reveal your presence to me.
Send your holy angels to encamp around my bed this night.
As I have tasted your gifts this day,
　　grant that I may enjoy them even more tomorrow.
I ask this through Jesus Christ, my Lord. Amen.

Mighty God,
　　you proclaim your Word of peace to the nations,
　　and you give salvation to those who live
　　　　according to your ways.
Open my ears that I may hear you more clearly.
Redeem my life from destruction throughout this night
　　and crown me with kindness and compassion.
I ask this in the name of Jesus Christ, your Son,
　　who lives and reigns with you and the Holy Spirit,
　　one God, for ever and ever. Amen.

All the ends of the earth have seen your salvation, O Lord.
Before I slip into a peaceful sleep,
　　I pause to praise you for your wondrous deeds
　　　　in my life today.
For all whom I have met
　　　　and with whom I have worked and played,
　　for all the food and drink you have set before me,
　　for all the safety you have provided,
　　I sing you this song of praise:
Glory be to you, Father, Son, and Holy Spirit,
　　one God, living for ever and ever. Amen.

Merciful God,
    nothing is lacking for those who follow your ways.
Great is your mercy before my eyes as I seek your truth.
Help me walk always in integrity.
Place my feet on the level ground of virtue.
Search my heart throughout this night
    and make me pleasing in your sight.
Grant this prayer through Jesus Christ, my Lord. Amen.

My help is in you, Lord, maker of heaven and earth.
You save me from my sins.
You heal my suffering and pain.
You protect me in times of distress.
For all your works I praise you.
This night I ask that you watch over me.
Lead me through a night of peaceful sleep
    to a new day of service in your presence.
Hear my prayer in the name of Jesus Christ, my Lord. Amen.

Lord Jesus Christ,
    you are the reflection of God's glory
    and the exact imprint of God's very being,
    sustaining all things by your powerful Word.
Shine your light of grace upon me throughout this night
    that I may sleep in peace and arise
        refreshed in your service.
You live and reign with the Father and the Holy Spirit,
    one God, for ever and ever. Amen.

Solemnities
and Feasts

JANUARY 1
MARY, MOTHER OF GOD

....

Abba, Father,
    in the fullness of time you sent your Son,
    born of the Virgin Mary, to save humankind.
As you once blessed the Mother of God,
    this night I ask you to bless and keep me,
    to let your face shine upon me and be gracious to me,
    to look upon me kindly and give me peace.
I utter this prayer in the name of Jesus,
    who is Lord for ever and ever. Amen.

JANUARY 25
CONVERSION OF ST. PAUL

....

Faithful God,
    in your plan to announce the gospel of your Son,
    you chose Saul and flooded his life with your light.
As your chosen instrument,
    Paul brought the good news to the nations
    so that your name would be glorified among all peoples.
Continue to convert me to your ways
    by guiding me with your Holy Spirit.
Keep me this night in your steadfast kindness.
I ask this in the name of Jesus Christ, my Lord,
    who lives and reigns with you and the Holy Spirit,
    one God, for ever and ever. Amen.

FEBRUARY 2
PRESENTATION OF THE LORD

All-powerful God,
    you are strong and mighty in your glory.
Through the presentation of your Son in the temple
    you have revealed your light to all the world.
Make me as righteous in my deeds
        as was your servant Simeon.
Make me as devout in my prayers
        as was your prophetess Anna.
Now may I go to sleep in peace
    for I have seen your salvation throughout this day
    manifested in the presence of Jesus Christ,
    who lives and reigns with you and the Holy Spirit,
    one God, for ever and ever. Amen.

FEBRUARY 22
CHAIR OF ST. PETER

Shepherd God,
    you never abandon your people,
    but lead them to the restful waters of baptism
    and spread the eucharistic table of your Son before them.
As once you chose Peter as the rock upon which
        to build your church,
    so have you continued to call shepherds
        to tend your sheep.
Grant to all your goodness and kindness.
Give me the courage tonight to declare, like Peter,
    that Jesus Christ is your Son.
You are the living God, Father, Son, and Holy Spirit,
    for ever and ever. Amen.

MARCH 19
ST. JOSEPH

My Father, my God, the rock, my savior,
  I sing your praises on this feast of St. Joseph,
  husband of the Blessed Virgin Mary.
The covenant sworn to David your servant
  was brought to fulfillment in the birth of your Son.
Trace in my life the righteousness of Joseph
  that I may do your will all the days of my life.
May all generations proclaim your faithfulness this night,
  Father, Son, and Holy Spirit,
  one God, for ever and ever. Amen.

MARCH 25
ANNUNCIATION OF THE LORD

Most High God,
  you gave your people the sign of the virgin with child
  in announcing the birth of my Lord Jesus Christ.
As you hailed your grace at work in Mary's obedience,
  stir up in me a willingness to do your will.
Grant that with the help of the Spirit
  I may announce your good news of salvation
  and reveal your kindness and your truth to all I meet.
May I rest secure this night
  knowing that you are Emmanuel, God with me,
  for ever and ever. Amen.

APRIL 25
ST. MARK

All-wise God,
 through your servant Mark
 you proclaimed the good news of Jesus Christ,
 crucified and raised from the dead.
Grant me a deeper understanding of your Word
 that I may more faithfully follow your Son.
 I join my voice with those of the ages
 singing of your favors and kindness
 and walking in the light of your countenance.
Wrap me in the cover of your fidelity this night.
All praise be yours, Father, Son, and Holy Spirit,
 for ever and ever. Amen.

MAY 3
STS. PHILIP AND JAMES

Father,
 the heavens declare your glory
 and the firmament proclaims your handiwork.
Your apostles Philip and James
 believed and announced the way, the truth, and the life
 of your Son, Jesus Christ.
Through all the earth their voices continue to resound
 as their message echoes to the ends of the earth.
As day has poured out your Word today,
 grant that this night will impart knowledge of your ways.
I ask this in the name of Jesus,
 who is Lord for ever and ever. Amen.

MAY 14
ST. MATTHIAS

God of heaven and earth,
from the rising of the sun to its setting
your name is worthy of all praise.
You chose Matthias from the world
to be an apostle of your Son.
Grant that even as you have chosen me through baptism
I may go forth and bear fruit in love.
Blessed be your name, Father, Son, and Holy Spirit,
this night and for ever and ever. Amen.

MAY 31
VISITATION OF THE BLESSED VIRGIN MARY

Great and holy God,
you have been my strength and courage this day.
You have made me confident and unafraid.
As Elizabeth's child leapt in her womb
at the sound of Mary's greeting,
may my heart rejoice within me
at the thought of all the great things
you have done for me.
I place all my trust in you this night, saving God,
through your Son, Jesus Christ,
in the unity of the Holy Spirit,
one God, for ever and ever. Amen.

JUNE 24
NATIVITY OF ST. JOHN THE BAPTIST

Most High God,
 before you formed me in my mother's womb you knew me.
Before I was born you dedicated me to your service.
I have depended on you from my birth for your strength.
Grant me the courage of John the Baptist
 that I may proclaim your justice and your salvation.
Always be my rock of refuge and stronghold of safety.
Fill me with peaceful rest this night.
I ask this in the name of Jesus Christ, my Lord. Amen.

JUNE 29
STS. PETER AND PAUL

Lord God,
 you founded your church on the apostles Peter and Paul,
 who proclaimed the death and resurrection of your Son.
Even as their message continues to resound
  through all the earth,
 grant that my voice may declare your love for all people.
Keep me faithful to my baptismal promises
 and give me a night of restful peace.
I ask this in the name of Jesus Christ,
 who lives and reigns with you and the Holy Spirit,
 one God, for ever and ever. Amen.

JULY 3
ST. THOMAS

Lord Jesus Christ,
   your apostle Thomas saw you and believed in you.
I have not seen you, yet I believe that you are present,
   protecting me and guiding me as your disciple.
Send me into the world with the good news
      of your resurrection
   after a night of restful trust in the fidelity of your Father,
   who lives and reigns with you and the Holy Spirit,
   one God, for ever and ever. Amen.

JULY 25
ST. JAMES

Creator God,
   you always do great things for your people.
You fill their earthen vessels with your powerful grace
   and trace in them the death and resurrection
      of your Son.
Your apostle James believed in Christ Jesus
   and drank from his cup of death and new life.
Grant that I may be worthy to serve you
   both in my waking and in my sleeping
   and give you thanks, Father, Son, and Holy Spirit,
   one God, for ever and ever. Amen.

AUGUST 6
THE TRANSFIGURATION

Ancient One,
    you are exalted throughout heaven and earth.
You reveal yourself in fire and cloud
    that all people may come to know your presence.
As you showed your glory through the transfiguration
      of your Son,
    so be pleased with my good works
    and conform me day by day into the image of Jesus Christ.
May your light shine throughout this night
    until the day dawns and the morning star rises in my heart.
Hear this prayer, Almighty Father, through your Son,
    who lives with you and the Holy Spirit,
      for ever and ever. Amen.

AUGUST 10
ST. LAWRENCE

Lord God,
    your servant Lawrence gave his life in imitation of Jesus.
Lavishly he gave to the poor,
    and now his generosity endures forever.
Like a grain of wheat falling to the earth and dying,
    he produced much fruit.
Give me a great love for your commands
    and move me to lend graciously and
      conduct my affairs with justice.
Keep me from walking in the darkness
    that I may share in the light of life of Jesus Christ,
    who lives and reigns with you and the Holy Spirit,
    one God, for ever and ever. Amen.

AUGUST 15
ASSUMPTION OF THE BLESSED VIRGIN MARY

Father of my Lord Jesus Christ,
  you have revealed the sign of the woman
    clothed with the sun,
  with the moon under her feet,
  and on her head a crown of twelve stars
  as the mother of your only-begotten Son.
As the new ark of your presence,
  she brought forth the anointed one
    who swallowed up death
  through his resurrection from the dead.
Mary already shares in Christ's victory over death;
  grant me a share in that life
  and take me to heaven to praise you eternally.
You are one God, Father, Son, and Holy Spirit,
  for ever and ever. Amen.

AUGUST 24
ST. BARTHOLOMEW

Just God,
  you reveal your holiness in all your works.
You are near to all who call upon you in truth.
Draw close to me throughout this night
  as once you revealed your presence
    to the apostle Bartholomew.
Grant that I may dream of your holy city
  coming down out of heaven
  that I may be united with your Son, the Lamb,
  who lives and reigns with you and the Holy Spirit,
  one God, for ever and ever. Amen.

AUGUST 29
MARTYRDOM OF ST. JOHN THE BAPTIST

Saving God,
 after he had fulfilled his mission of
  preparing the world for your Son,
 John the Baptist gave his life to honor your name.
His memory lives in the hearts of those who serve you.
Inspire me with the words that herald your righteousness.
Strengthen my dependence upon your grace
 and help me fulfill my mission in the world.
Let me sleep in the stronghold of your safety
 for you are my hope, my rock, and my fortress.
Hear my prayer in the name of Jesus Christ, my Lord. Amen.

SEPTEMBER 8
NATIVITY OF THE BLESSED VIRGIN MARY

Mighty God,
 all things work for good for those who love you.
From before her birth,
 you called the Blessed Virgin Mary
  to be the mother of your Son.
The virgin of Nazareth delighted in your name
 and willingly trusted in your mercy.
Throughout this night
 make my heart rejoice in the salvation you have brought
 through your Son, Jesus Christ,
 who is Lord for ever and ever. Amen.

SEPTEMBER 14
EXALTATION OF THE HOLY CROSS

Jesus Christ,
  though you were in the form of God,
  you did not regard equality with God something
    to be grasped.
You emptied yourself in human likeness
  and humbled yourself through your death on the cross.
Thus, you redeemed the world.
This night I join my voice with those of every time and place
  who confess you as Lord to the glory of God the Father
  in the unity of the Holy Spirit,
    one God, for ever and ever. Amen.

SEPTEMBER 21
ST. MATTHEW

Father of all,
  you are over all and through all and in all.
Through the ministry of your apostle and evangelist Matthew
  you have called all people to one faith and one baptism.
Help me live in a manner worthy of the call I have received
  with all humility and gentleness and patience.
Help me preserve the unity of the Spirit
  through the bond of peace.
Deepen my awareness that I am a member
    of the one body of Christ
    that the grace he has measured out to me
    may accomplish the work you have given me.
This night I praise you, Father, Son, and Holy Spirit,
  one God, living for ever and ever. Amen.

SEPTEMBER 29
STS. MICHAEL, GABRIEL, AND RAPHAEL

Ancient One,
> you choose both visible and invisible ministers
> to serve you, to praise you, and to do your will.

Michael reminds me of your presence.
Gabriel reminds me of your strength.
Raphael reminds me of your healing power.
May I strive to serve you on earth
> as your archangels serve you in heaven.

Hear my prayer of thanksgiving this night,
> Father, Son, and Holy Spirit.

May you be praised for ever and ever. Amen.

OCTOBER 18
ST. LUKE

Lord God,
> you are just in all your ways
> and you are near to those who call upon you in truth.

Your evangelist Luke shared the splendor of your kingdom
> through his gospel revealing the glory of your Son.

After a night of rest,
> send me as a laborer into the harvest
> that I might proclaim the good news of salvation
> to the ends of the world.

Hear my prayer in the name of Jesus Christ, my Lord. Amen.

OCTOBER 28
STS. SIMON AND JUDE

Lord Jesus Christ,
>through your death and resurrection
>you have made me your follower
>with your apostles Simon and Jude.
Keep me as a faithful member of your Father's household.
Give me a full night of peaceful sleep
>that I may proclaim your name
>along with the Father and the Holy Spirit
>to the ends of world,
>now and for ever and ever. Amen.

NOVEMBER 1
ALL SAINTS

Father,
Through the living waters of baptism
>you have united your children
>as a people from every nation, race, and tongue.
As I remember all your saints this night,
>keep me faithful to my baptismal promises.
Mark me with the seal of your enduring love.
When my journey here is complete,
>welcome me into your kingdom
>where the poor in spirit, the mourners, the meek,
>the merciful, the clean of heart, and the peacemakers
>see you as you are:
Father, Son, and Holy Spirit, one God, for ever and ever.
Amen.

NOVEMBER 2
ALL SOULS

God of all life,
 through the death and resurrection of your Son
 you have destroyed death forever,
 and you have removed the veil covering all people,
 and the web woven over all nations.
You have wiped away all tears
 from the faces of those who trust in you.
Precious in your eyes is the death of your faithful ones.
This night as I remember all my relatives
  and friends who have died,
 grant me the trust that I may one day
  dwell in your house.
May the weeping that comes with nightfall
 be followed by rejoicing at dawn.
Hear this prayer in the name of Jesus Christ,
 who lives and reigns with you and the Holy Spirit,
 one God, for ever and ever. Amen.

NOVEMBER 9
DEDICATION OF THE LATERAN BASILICA IN ROME

Lord Jesus Christ,
    you are the cornerstone of the church.
Upon you rises the temple of your people
    in whom dwells the Holy Spirit.
Be my refuge and strength this night,
    and let me not be disturbed.
As I remember the dedication
    of the mother of all your churches,
      let me sleep secure knowing that you will be with me
        at the break of dawn.
Bring my prayer to the Father with whom you live and reign
    in the unity of the Holy Spirit, one God,
      for ever and ever. Amen.

NOVEMBER 30
ST. ANDREW

God of spirit and life,
 you have made beautiful the feet
 of those who bring your good news to your people.
Throughout the world this night
 your church gives you thanks for the apostle Andrew,
 one who became a fisher of people
 at the invitation of your Son, my Lord Jesus Christ.
Grant that as I confess with my mouth that Jesus is Lord,
 I may believe in my heart that
  you have raised him from the dead
 and this night experience the salvation he won for me.
Hear my prayer through your Holy Spirit,
 who lives and reigns with you and Jesus Christ,
 one God, for ever and ever. Amen.

FOURTH THURSDAY IN NOVEMBER
THANKSGIVING DAY

Giver of all good gifts,
 you foster my growth from the womb
 and fashion me according to your will.
You journey with me throughout my life,
 leading me and guiding me,
 providing me with food and shelter and clothing.
This night I give you thanks for all the countless gifts
 that you have bestowed upon me.
May your name be praised
 from the rising of the sun to its setting
 for you are one God, Father, Son, and Holy Spirit,
 for ever and ever. Amen.

DECEMBER 8
IMMACULATE CONCEPTION
OF THE BLESSED VIRGIN MARY

Father of my Lord Jesus Christ,
  you have blessed me in him,
  born of the immaculate Virgin,
  with every spiritual blessing in the heavens.
You chose Blessed Mary to be his mother
  before the foundation of the world
  to be holy and without blemish.
All the ends of the earth have seen your salvation.
This night I praise your wondrous deeds
  even as I ask you to accomplish in me
    the intention of your will
  that all I do might give you glory.
Hear my prayer in the name of your Son,
  who lives and reigns with you and the Holy Spirit,
  one God, for ever and ever. Amen.

DECEMBER 12
OUR LADY OF GUADALUPE

God of heaven and earth,
  you revealed your sign
  of the woman clothed with the sun,
  with the moon under her feet,
  and on her head a crown of twelve stars.
Through the prayers of Our Lady of Guadalupe
  grant me a restful night in your presence.
May you be blessed through the Virgin Mary
  through whom came our salvation in Jesus Christ,
  who is Lord for ever and ever. Amen.

DECEMBER 26
ST. STEPHEN

God of light,
    your faithful follower Stephen
    gave his life as a witness to your Son.
Into your hands he commended his spirit
    in the hope of resurrection from the dead.
Strengthen my faith and help me bear witness to you.
Into your hands I commend my spirit this night.
Hear my prayer through Jesus Christ, my Lord. Amen.

DECEMBER 27
ST. JOHN THE EVANGELIST

Father,
    your beloved servant John
    in the glorious company of the apostles of your Son,
    proclaimed the eternal life that was made visible in Jesus.
As I continue to celebrate the birth of Jesus Christ,
    strengthen my fellowship with you and him
    and your Holy Spirit throughout this night.
Hear this prayer of praise through your Word of Life,
    who is Lord for ever and ever. Amen.

DECEMBER 28
HOLY INNOCENTS

I praise you, God, creator of heaven and earth,
    and I acclaim you as Lord.
Your light shatters the darkness.
Like the Holy Innocents and all your martyrs,
    may I reveal the presence of your Son
    through my heroic witness of faith.
I long to join the ranks of that white-robed army
    that praises your name in heaven.
Free me from the terrors of this night
    and help me walk always in the light
    of Jesus Christ, who is Lord for ever and ever. Amen.

YOUR OWN BIRTHDAY

Lord God,
    you formed my inmost being,
        knitting me in my mother's womb.
On you I have depended from birth;
    from my youth I have trusted you.
As I celebrate this _____ year of my life,
    bless me and guide me
    that I may gain wisdom of heart.
Be my strength this night.
I ask this in the name of Jesus, my Lord. Amen.

Night Prayer

Formerly called Compline, Night Prayer is the final prayer of the day for those who use the Liturgy of the Hours. It is prayed immediately before going to bed, either by the individual alone or by members of a community (family, monastery, convent, secular institute, etc.). Following is a simple outline for those who might like to try this prayer. All you need is a Bible. The leader or person praying begins with the following verse:

Leader: God, come to my assistance.
All: Lord, make haste to help me.
Leader: Glory to the Father, and to the Son, and to the Holy Spirit
All: as it was in the beginning, is now, and will be for ever. Amen.

Now pause for a brief examination of conscience, followed by a penitential prayer, for example, "I confess to almighty God...." Now read the appropriate psalm(s) and reading, as indicated below:

Sunday: Psalm 91, Revelation 22:4–5
Monday: Psalm 86, 1 Thessalonians 5:9–10
Tuesday: Psalm 143:1–11, 1 Peter 5:8–9a
Wednesday: Psalms 31:1–6 & 130, Ephesians 4:26–27
Thursday: Psalm 16, 1 Thessalonians 5:23
Friday: Psalm 88, Jeremiah 14:9a
Saturday: Psalms 4 & 134, Deuteronomy 6:4–7

At the end of each psalm, add the "Glory to the Father..." as indicated above. After the psalm(s) and the brief Scripture reading, recite Simeon's Canticle (Luke 2:29–32) and the "Glory to the Father...." Then say a concluding prayer from among those in this book. The prayer is followed by this blessing:

Leader: May the all-powerful Lord grant us a restful night and a peaceful death.
All: Amen.

Finally, recite or sing a prayer in honor of the Blessed Virgin Mary. This can be the "Hail, Holy Queen," the "Hail Mary," or another Marian prayer or hymn.